To the people of Huntsville, and all those who seek freedom and justice through peace.
With gratitude to Beck McDowell, for service above and beyond.
And with appreciation to Leslie Holder, for making my Moondream come true.
H. B.

To Bernadette Santiago (my Dette)
E. B. L.

The author acknowledges with gratitude the invaluable assistance provided in the creation of this book by
Dr. Sonnie W. Hereford III, Sonnie W. Hereford IV, Beck McDowell, Laurel Best, Ann Marie Martin,
Heather Montgomery, Henry Kyemba, Susanna Leberman, the Huntsville-Madison County Public Library,
Mike Chappell, Dr. Waymon E. Burke, Ann Neely, and the 3Skillets/Sandwich Farm restaurant.

Original historical photographs were graciously permitted to be utilized as reference material
for the original watercolor illustrations appearing on pages 24 and 27 by the Center for the Study
of Southern Political Culture Archive at Calhoun Community College, Research Park Campus,
in Huntsville, Alabama; Waymon E. Burke, PhD, Project Director.

Author's Note photos by Henry M. Kyemba Jr.

First edition 2015

Library of Congress Catalog Card Number 2013955948
ISBN 978-0-7636-6919-5

14 15 16 17 18 19 CCP 10 9 8 7 6 5 4 3 2 1

Printed in Shenzhen, Guangdong, China

This book was typeset in Fairfield Medium.
The illustrations were done in watercolor.

Candlewick Press
99 Dover Street
Somerville, Massachusetts 02144

visit us at www.candlewick.com

SEEDS OF FREEDOM

The Peaceful Integration of Huntsville, Alabama

HESTER BASS

illustrated by E. B. LEWIS

CANDLEWICK PRESS

JANUARY 1962

Life is good in the mountains of north Alabama. Huntsville is the "Space Center of the Universe." German scientists, enemies of the United States just twenty years before, are working peacefully beside American engineers. Rockets that will take astronauts to the moon are sprouting beside the cotton fields. But these aren't good times for everyone.

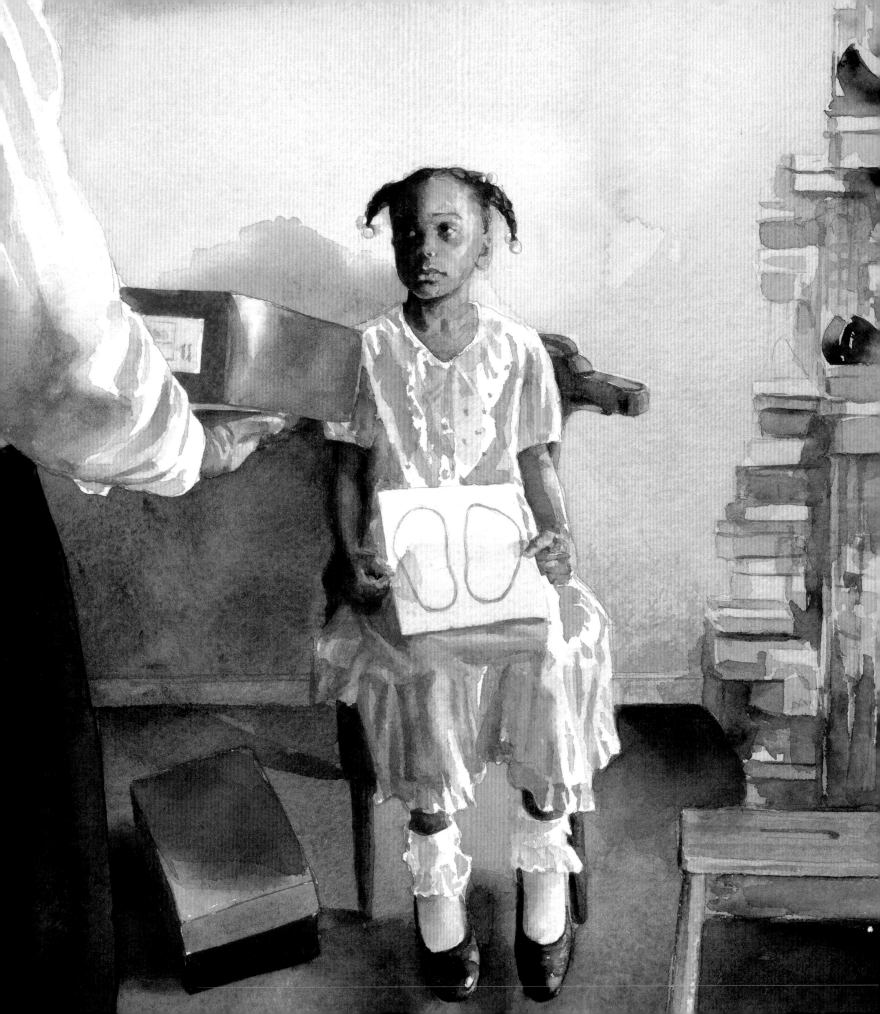

A girl carries paper pictures of her feet because she won't be allowed to try on shoes. A boy wants to read but cannot use the public library. And a family tries to eat in a restaurant, but the owner locks the door in their faces.

Huntsville has escaped the violence that has divided some cities into black and white. However, like a lot of places in America, there are invisible lines not to be crossed.

But change is in the air. Segregation—keeping people separate because of the color of their skin—is on the way out. It's time to bring people together. Time to plan. Time for action.

Time to sow the seeds of freedom.

Young black men and women — students — sit at lunch counters in the stores downtown. They have money and can buy anything in the store, except lunch. Can't use the restrooms either.

Just the way it is.

These students know they will be asked to leave. Know that if they don't, they'll go to jail. But they sit at these lunch counters, day after day. It's called a sit-in, a nonviolent gesture against "just the way it is."

The seeds of freedom are planted in Huntsville. What will it take to make them grow?

As the first American astronaut circles in orbit around the Earth, black men, women, and children circle around the courthouse, wearing signs that say things like *I Ordered a Hamburger. They Served Me a Warrant!* (Meaning they were arrested.) *Hungry for Justice?* (They certainly were.) *Children Like Freedom, Too!* (Exactly.)

But walking in circles day after day makes them weary of waiting for change. The seeds of freedom need inspiration to grow. So a man of peace is invited to Huntsville. A man not very well known. Not yet.

Dr. Martin Luther King Jr. speaks of a time to come when black children and white children will join hands as brothers and sisters. People cheer and rise to their feet. But there's not much in the Huntsville newspaper about it, or about anything else that's happening with the civil rights movement in town. Reporters seem to agree that segregation is "just the way it is," and that if they keep quiet, maybe all these protests will just go away. But the seeds of freedom need attention to grow. So three women decide to do something risky.

They sit down to have lunch together. A college student, a doctor's wife about to have a child, and the wife of a dentist with a baby girl in her arms. They are quiet and respectful, but because they are black, they are asked to leave. They don't. The police, who don't want this trouble, ask the ladies to go home. They won't. So the police reluctantly arrest all three of them—four including the baby.

It's hard to keep it quiet when a baby goes to jail. Magazines across the nation report this story, sending a wave of worry across Huntsville. The "Rocket City" depends on money from the American government to stay busy with the space program, and this kind of news is bad for business. But the seeds of freedom need news to grow, so another plan is hatched.

The people of Huntsville, black and white, usually did a lot of shopping for Easter. Clothes. Hats. Shoes. A new outfit could cost a hundred dollars. So the black leaders of Huntsville ask the black people of the whole county to keep a secret. *Shhh.* They will stand up for freedom by dressing down.

Huntsville will have a Blue Jean Sunday. In 1962, only farmers wear blue jeans, and most women do not wear pants at all. Plus, such a public protest could be dangerous. People might call you names. Try to hurt you. Threaten to take your home, your job, your life.

But the black citizens of north Alabama know that money can talk, so they go out of town, even out of state, to buy five-dollar blue jeans instead of fancy clothes. Some women buy denim fabric and make skirts.

Store owners notice when all those new clothes go unsold. Some people think Huntsville merchants lose about a million dollars. Blue Jean Sunday is rich encouragement for the seeds of freedom. A little fresh air and sunshine might just do the trick.

The public parks in Huntsville are for whites only, but a few black citizens decide to spend Mother's Day downtown in Big Spring Park. The children swing and slide and ride the merry-go-round. People stare, but no one asks them to leave. And ducks don't care what color hand feeds them.

About a week later, a man is speaking on the courthouse steps, campaigning to be governor. George Wallace. He says black and white people should be separated everywhere. Now. Tomorrow. Forever.

The black people of Huntsville have a different message. They ride around the courthouse square in the back of a truck. Waving flags. Playing patriotic music. Holding balloons filled with helium and tied with notes that say things like *Please Support Freedom in Huntsville*. They let all the balloons go until the sky is dotted with color. Wherever each balloon lands, it will plant a tiny seed of freedom.

Across the country, the call for change is heard. President John F. Kennedy supports freedom for all Americans. It is the law for buses, trains, and public schools to be open to everyone, although that is not yet the case.

Huntsville is prosperous, proud, peaceful. To keep it that way, the mayor realizes that whatever threatens the future of Huntsville must be stopped—even if it means stopping nearly a century of custom and tradition and "just the way it is."

JULY 1962

Only six months after the first Huntsville sit-in, victory is in sight. Black civil rights leaders and white city officials convince downtown business owners to integrate—to bring Huntsville's black and white citizens together—in peace. No one wants anyone who might turn this into a violent confrontation to know about the plan, so it's kept secret. *Shhh.*

On a certain day at certain lunch counters, a certain time arrives. Black men and women sit down and have lunch beside white men and women. Some ask, "Is this okay?" Lunch counter servers say, "This is what we're doing, right?" Policemen out of uniform keep watch, but there's no trouble.

Over the summer, little by little, people come together. At the hospital. The bowling alley. The movie theater. The tender plant of freedom is growing. But not in the schools.

In the fall, President Kennedy visits Huntsville to see the rockets and talk about freedom. Thirty-five black families ask the school board to obey the law that makes separate schools illegal. But the school board does nothing. Angry voices on the telephone threaten these families until only four agree to be part of a lawsuit, which won't be heard by a judge for nearly a year. Meanwhile, schools for black children have no library, no cafeteria, and no buses while the schools for white children seem to have everything. Are the seeds of freedom wilting?

It's a peaceful spring and summer in Huntsville in 1963, but not elsewhere in Alabama. More than a thousand black children gather for a nonviolent protest in a Birmingham park. They are met with gushing fire hoses and snarling dogs.

It's on television, nationwide.

The man who wanted segregation forever is now governor. He stands in the university door, trying to keep black students out.

It's on television, nationwide.

Two hundred thousand people march for freedom in Washington, D.C. Dr. King gives a speech, echoing the dream that black children and white children will join hands in peace.

It's on television, nationwide.

In the heat of August, four Huntsville families face the judge. Since the law is clear, he rules quickly, saying, "Admit these four students to school."

SEPTEMBER 1963

On the Tuesday after Labor Day, families all over Huntsville are packing satchels with pencils and paper. Four black children prepare to walk into history, each hand in hand with a parent, each approaching a school where no friends are waiting. People shout ugly words at them. There are reporters, photographers. Four hands reach for doors . . . that are locked.

Governor Wallace has closed all Alabama public schools planning to admit black students. Across town, at a private religious school with all black students, twelve white students begin school without incident, in the first case of so-called reverse integration in Alabama.

By Friday, Wallace sends state troopers to greet anyone trying to go to public school in Huntsville with weapons and helmets and stern, grim faces. To keep the peace, he says.

On Monday, September 9, the students are ready to try again. The crowds and troopers are gone. There are a few city policemen, reporters, photographers—and children just trying to go to school.

At about eight thirty that morning, Dr. Sonnie W. Hereford III, a leader in the civil rights movement, walks into Fifth Avenue School with his six-year-old son, Sonnie W. Hereford IV, who becomes the first black child to attend a formerly all-white public school in the state of Alabama.

Another peaceful first for Huntsville.

There will be more work ahead, but through nonviolence and dignity and cooperation and courage, the black and white people of Huntsville have come together in peace, to taste the sweet fruit homegrown from the seeds of freedom.

AUTHOR'S NOTE

I lived in Huntsville, Alabama, for ten years and came to this story through two historical markers, noting that the first instances of both an integrated public school and a "reverse-integrated" private school happened in Huntsville in the same week of September 1963. My mind raced with the "how" and "why" of these events.

FIFTH AVENUE SCHOOL
Site of Alabama's First Public School Integration

Opened in 1944, the Fifth Avenue School became the focal point for major educational change on September 9, 1963, when Sonnie Hereford IV became the first African-American student to integrate public schools in Alabama. Following a lengthy court battle, Dr. Sonnie Hereford III enrolled his son in the first grade at the school. Veronica Pearson (Rison School), David (Piggee) Osman (Terry Heights School), and John Anthony Brewton (East Clinton School) enrolled in other Huntsville City Schools later that day. Other Alabama school systems began desegregation in the weeks that followed. The school was razed in 2003.

SPONSORED BY HUNTSVILLE PUBLIC SCHOOL, COLLEGE AND UNIVERSITY FOUNDATIONS & FRIENDS 2004

ST. JOSEPH'S MISSION SCHOOL

The first integrated elementary education classes in the state of Alabama took place quietly and peacefully here September 3, 1963.

St. Joseph's Mission, church and school, was founded by the Society of the Divine Savior (Salvatorians) to serve the African American community of Madison County. In early fall of 1963, twelve white students submitted applications and were accepted for admission. The event is noted not only for the initial integration of elementary schools in Alabama but also for its "reverse" integration nature.

In 1979, St. Joseph's School merged with St. Mary's School and the combined school, named Holy Family School, continues to operate on this site.

"Religion along with education... that's the reason it works."
Rev. Mark Sterbenz, S.D.S. (Pastor, St. Joseph's Mission, 1961-1967)

ERECTED 1994 BY ST. JOSEPH CATHOLIC COMMUNITY

This story started a long time ago, rooted in slavery.

The practice of a person being bought, sold, or owned by another person has existed for thousands of years, in many parts of the world, probably ever since there was a war, a crime, a debt, or simply a job that someone did not want to do. Whenever one group of people sees another group of people as lesser than themselves, prejudice and discrimination and enslavement can follow. Even now, in the twenty-first century, slavery exists.

In America, as soon as the explorers and colonists landed, the struggle for civil rights began. Native people were already living here. And while many groups of people have suffered from injustice in this country, the focus here is on the journey of African Americans from slavery toward freedom.

From the beginning of this nation, states could pass laws—the Slave Codes, starting in the mid-1600s, and the Black Codes, dating from the early-to-mid-1800s—to regulate the privileges of African Americans. Later, in many states, so-called Jim Crow laws were in effect from 1876 to 1965 to keep black people and white people separate in all kinds of ways—on buses and trains, in schools and hospitals, in restaurants and theaters, in parks and pools—nearly everywhere—making segregation legal.

Efforts had been made to keep this from happening, during and especially after the Civil War. In 1863, President Abraham Lincoln signed the Emancipation Proclamation, stating that when federal forces took control of states that had seceded from the Union, all slaves there would be recognized as free, but it did not apply in the border states and it did not outlaw slavery. In 1865, the Thirteenth Amendment to the U.S. Constitution abolished slavery. In 1868, the Fourteenth Amendment declared that all American citizens, including former slaves, were to receive equal protection under the law and that no state could deny this right to any citizen. In 1870, the Fifteenth Amendment stated that no African-American man would be denied the right to vote because of his race or color. But this was not enough.

There have been several Civil Rights Acts, passed as early as 1866, intended to protect the liberties of African-American citizens. One proposed in 1875 prohibited discrimination in facilities open to the public but was struck down as unconstitutional in 1883 by the U.S. Supreme Court, which ruled that social rights in privately owned businesses were not the same as civil rights and therefore were not protected by the Fourteenth Amendment.

Then came the landmark Louisiana case *Plessy v. Ferguson,* upheld by the U.S. Supreme Court in 1896, which established the legal practice of "separate but equal" facilities for people with light skin, called white or Caucasian, and people with dark skin, called black or colored or Negro—or worse. People of mixed race were considered "colored" no matter what the shade of their skin.

During the hundred years from the Civil War to the 1960s, things in the black and white world of America were certainly separate, but rarely if ever equal. This was especially true in the American South, but it was true elsewhere in the United States as well, and would not be legally refuted until the U.S. Supreme Court ruled in *Brown v. Board of Education of Topeka* in 1954 that segregated schools were unconstitutional. It took the Civil Rights Act of 1964, the Voting Rights Act of 1965, and the Fair Housing Act of 1968 to further correct the injustices of the past.

But no law can erase bitterness and hatred and custom and tradition. That takes time and effort and the will of the people. What sets Huntsville apart, in my mind, was the commitment on both sides to face integration without violence. This was not the case in many communities.

Still, Huntsville's record was not spotless. There were incidents of shoving and name-calling at the sit-ins. One protester discovered too late that his car seat had been smeared with mustard oil and his skin was chemically burned. And the psychological effects of being denied basic human rights were sharply hurtful. But there were no riots, no white tanks, and no bombs in Huntsville. The images of racial violence that were burned into the memories of anyone who saw them occurred elsewhere.

Ultimately, economics provided the wedge of change for Huntsville. White leaders did not want to lose federal space-program contracts, and black leaders recognized their financial leverage through protests outside the stock exchanges in New York and Chicago, asking people not to invest in a segregated city, as well as such events as Blue Jean Sunday.

What happened next?

On Sunday, September 15, 1963 — less than a week after the peaceful public school integration in Huntsville — the Sixteenth Street Baptist Church in Birmingham, Alabama, was bombed. Four girls were killed, twenty-one people were injured, and two boys died in the violence that followed.

President Kennedy never saw one of those Huntsville rockets send a man to the moon. He was killed on November 22, 1963. The Civil Rights Act he championed was signed into law by President Lyndon Johnson on July 2, 1964.

As of this writing, the public schools in Huntsville still operate under a federal desegregation order stemming from the 1962 lawsuit. Many other school systems in several states are in similar situations. These schools are officially integrated, but often neighborhoods retain traditional racial boundaries, meaning that some schools still serve mostly white children and others mostly black children. The struggle continues.

Sometimes change comes slowly. Sometimes change comes all at once. But change usually comes when someone decides that enough is enough. That's what happened in Huntsville. That's what is still happening across America and throughout the world. Sometimes all it takes is one person to start something good. In your community, that person could be you.

SELECTED BIBLIOGRAPHY

Books about the Civil Rights Movement in Huntsville

Cashin, Sheryll. *The Agitator's Daughter: A Memoir of Four Generations of One Extraordinary African-American Family*. New York: PublicAffairs, 2008.

Hereford, Sonnie Wellington III, and Jack D. Ellis. *Beside the Troubled Waters: A Black Doctor Remembers Life, Medicine, and Civil Rights in an Alabama Town*. Tuscaloosa: University of Alabama Press, 2011.

Books for Children about the Civil Rights Movement

Bridges, Ruby. *Through My Eyes*. New York: Scholastic, 1999.

Brimner, Larry Dane. *Birmingham Sunday*. Honesdale, PA: Calkins Creek, 2010.

———. *Black & White: The Confrontation between Reverend Fred L. Shuttlesworth and Eugene "Bull" Connor*. Honesdale, PA: Calkins Creek, 2011.

Haskins, James. *Delivering Justice: W.W. Law and the Fight for Civil Rights*. Illustrated by Benny Andrews. Cambridge, MA: Candlewick Press, 2005.

Levine, Ellen. *Freedom's Children: Young Civil Rights Activists Tell Their Own Stories*. New York: Puffin, 1994.

Morrison, Toni. *Remember: The Journey to School Integration*. Boston: Houghton Mifflin, 2004.

Pinkney, Andrea Davis. *Sit-in: How Four Friends Stood Up by Sitting Down*. Illustrated by Brian Pinkney. New York: Little, Brown, 2010.

Weatherford, Carole Boston. *Birmingham, 1963*. Honesdale, PA: Wordsong, 2007.

———. *Freedom on the Menu: The Greensboro Sit-ins*. Illustrated by Jerome Lagarrigue. New York: Dial, 2005.

Books about the Civil Rights Movement

Gaillard, Frye, Jennifer Lindsay, and Jane DeNeefe. *Alabama's Civil Rights Trail: An Illustrated Guide to the Cradle of Freedom*. Tuscaloosa: University of Alabama Press, 2010.

Williams, Juan. *Eyes on the Prize: America's Civil Rights Years, 1954–1965*. New York: Viking, 1987, 2002.